# Wolfgang Amadeus MOZART

(1756 – 1791)

## Concerto for Piano and Orchestra, KV 415
## C Major / Ut majeur / C-Dur

Piano Reduction

DOWANI International

# Preface

With this edition we offer you Wolfgang Amadeus Mozart's Piano Concerto No. 13 in C Major K. 415, which was composed in Vienna in 1782/83. The piece is notable for its brilliance and is moderately difficult. Our edition enables you to work your way through the piece systematically and in three different tempi with professional accompaniment.

On the first CD (CD A) you can listen to the concert version of each movement (piano with orchestra) and also find the slow tempo-version of the accompaniment of each movement. On the second CD (CD B) you can hear the accompaniments of all of the movements at a moderate tempo and the orchestral accompaniment at the original tempo to play along to. The piano reduction of the orchestral part is played by a professional coach. When you begin to practice this piece, start at the slow tempo. If your stereo system is equipped with a balance control, you can place either the solo piano or the piano accompaniment in the foreground by adjusting the control. In the middle position, both pianos can be heard at the same volume. If you do not have a balance control, you can listen to each part on a separate loudspeaker. After you have studied the concerto in the slow tempo, you can advance to the intermediate tempo and refine your playing. Having mastered this practice tempo, you can now advance to the original tempo with orchestral accompaniment. At both the middle and original tempi, the piano or orchestral accompaniment can be heard on both channels (without solo piano) in stereo quality. Each movement has been sensibly divided into subsections for practice purposes. You can select the subsection you want using the track numbers indicated in the solo part.

As an aid to ensemble playing with the pianist and the orchestra, the passages where the solo piano plays unaccompanied come with metronome clicks in the background to help you stay in the right tempo. The cadenzas and solo entrances are only played out completely in the concert version. In the practice tempo-versions you can find your entry after the cadenzas and solo entrances with the help of the metronome clicks mentioned above, or by pressing the pause button of your CD-player before the cadenzas and solo entrances and then selecting the next track number to continue playing. The cadenzas are written out in this edition, as they are original cadenzas written by Mozart himself. Further explanations can be found at the end of this volume along with the names of the musicians involved in the recording. More detailed information can be found in the Internet at www.dowani.com. All of the versions were recorded live.

Piano teaching has made enormous progress in recent years. Many piano teachers have their own ideas, theories and experiences, especially in matters of fingering and the use of the pedal. We therefore deliberately refrain from adding fingering or pedaling marks to our piano editions.

We wish you lots of fun playing from our *DOWANI 3 Tempi Play Along* editions and hope that your musicality and diligence will enable you to play the concert version as soon as possible. It is our goal to give you the essential conditions for effective practicing through motivation, enjoyment and fun.

Your DOWANI Team

# Avant-propos

La présente édition vous propose le concerto pour piano KV 415 en Ut majeur de Wolfgang Amadeus Mozart, composé en 1782/83 à Vienne. D'un caractère très brillant, cette œuvre est moyennement difficile. Notre édition vous permet de travailler le concerto de manière systématique en trois vitesses différentes avec un accompagnement professionnel.

Vous trouverez sur le premier CD (CD A) la version de concert de chacun des mouvements (piano avec orchestre) destinée à l'écoute, ainsi que l'accompagnement de tous les mouvements au tempo lent. Le deuxième CD (CD B) contient l'accompagnement au tempo moyen et l'accompagnement d'orchestre au tempo original pour jouer avec. La réduction pour piano de la partie d'orchestre sera jouée par un répétiteur professionnel. Votre premier contact avec le morceau devrait se faire à un tempo lent. Si votre chaîne hi-fi dispose d'un réglage de balance, vous pouvez l'utiliser pour mettre au premier plan soit le piano solo, soit l'accompagne-

ment de piano. En équilibrant la balance, vous entendrez les deux pianos à volume égal. Si vous ne disposez pas de réglage de balance, vous entendrez chacun des pianos sur un des haut-parleurs. Après avoir étudié le morceau à un tempo lent, vous pourrez améliorer votre jeu à un tempo modéré. Si vous maîtrisez également ce tempo de travail, vous pourrez jouer le tempo original avec accompagnement d'orchestre. Dans ces deux tempos – modéré et original – vous entendrez l'accompagnement de piano ou d'orchestre sur les deux canaux en stéréo (sans la partie soliste). Chaque mouvement a été divisé en sections judicieuses pour faciliter le travail. Vous pouvez sélectionner ces sections à l'aide des numéros de plages indiqués dans la partie du soliste. Afin de garantir le meilleur jeu d'ensemble possible avec le répétiteur et l'orchestre et de garder le bon tempo plus facilement, vous entendrez à l'arrière-plan le battement du métronome dans les passages où le piano soliste joue sans accompagnement. Les cadences et entrées ne seront jouées complètement que dans la version de concert. Dans les vitesses d'entraînement vous trouverez les départs après les cadences et entrées à l'aide des clics de métronome mentionnés ci-dessus ou bien en arrêtant votre lecteur de CD avec la touche "Pause" avant les cadences et entrées et en continuant la lecture au début de la plage suivante. Les cadences étant celles de Mozart, elles ont été intégrées dans la partition. Pour obtenir plus d'informations et les noms des artistes qui ont participé aux enregistrements, veuillez consulter la dernière page de cette édition ou notre site Internet : www.dowani.com. Toutes les versions ont été enregistrées en direct.

La pédagogie instrumentale pour le piano a beaucoup progressé au cours des dernières années. Beaucoup de professeurs

de piano ont leurs propres idées, leurs théories et leurs expériences – surtout en ce qui concerne les doigtés et l'utilisation de la pédale. C'est la raison pour laquelle nous avons délibérément renoncé à indiquer les doigtés et les signes pour la pédale.

Nous vous souhaitons beaucoup de plaisir à faire de la musique avec la collection *DOWANI 3 Tempi Play Along* et nous espérons que votre musicalité et votre application vous amèneront aussi rapidement que possible à la version de concert. Notre but est de vous offrir les bases nécessaires pour un travail efficace par la motivation et le plaisir.

Les Éditions DOWANI

# Vorwort

Mit der vorliegenden Ausgabe präsentieren wir Ihnen Wolfgang Amadeus Mozarts Klavierkonzert KV 415 in C-Dur, welches 1782/83 in Wien entstanden ist. Das Werk ist sehr brillant und hat einen mittleren Schwierigkeitsgrad. Unsere Ausgabe ermöglicht es Ihnen, das Werk systematisch und in drei verschiedenen Tempi mit professioneller Begleitung zu erarbeiten.

Auf der ersten CD (CD A) finden Sie die Konzertversion eines jeden Satzes (Klavier mit Orchester) zum Anhören sowie die Begleitung aller Sätze im langsamen Tempo. Auf der zweiten CD (CD B) hören Sie die Begleitung aller Sätze im mittleren Tempo und die Orchesterbegleitung im originalen Tempo zum Mitspielen. Den Klavierauszug des Orchesterparts übernimmt ein professioneller Korrepetitor. Ihr erster Übe-Kontakt mit dem Stück sollte im langsamen Tempo stattfinden. Wenn Ihre Stereoanlage über einen Balance-Regler verfügt, können Sie im langsamen Tempo durch Drehen des Reglers entweder das Solo-Klavier oder die Klavierbegleitung stufenlos in den Vordergrund blenden. In der Mittelposition erklingen beide Klaviere gleich laut. Falls Sie keinen Balance-Regler haben, hören Sie jedes Klavier jeweils auf einem Lautsprecher. Nachdem Sie das Stück im langsamen Tempo einstudiert haben, können Sie Ihr Spiel im mittleren Tempo verfeinern. Wenn Sie auch dieses Übe-Tempo beherrschen, können Sie mit Orchester im originalen Tempo musizieren. Die Klavier- bzw. Orchesterbegleitung erklingt im mittleren und originalen Tempo auf beiden Kanälen in Stereo-Qualität (ohne Solo-Klavier). Jeder Satz wurde in sinnvolle Übe-Abschnitte unterteilt. Diese können Sie mit Hilfe der in der Solostimme angegebenen Track-Nummern auswählen. Damit

ein optimales Zusammenspiel mit dem Korrepetitor und dem Orchester gewährleistet ist, hören Sie an den Stellen, an denen das Soloklavier ohne Begleitung spielt, als Orientierungshilfe Metronomklicks im Hintergrund, um im richtigen Tempo zu bleiben. Die Kadenzen und Eingänge werden nur in der Konzertversion komplett gespielt. Bei den Übe-Tempi finden Sie den Einsatz nach den Kadenzen und Eingängen mit Hilfe der oben erwähnten Metronomklicks oder indem Sie vor den Kadenzen und Eingängen die Pausentaste des CD-Players drücken und bei der nächsten Tracknummer weiterspielen. Die Kadenzen wurden in dieser Ausgabe notiert, da es sich um originale Kadenzen von Mozart handelt. Weitere Erklärungen sowie die Namen der Künstler finden Sie auf der letzten Seite dieser Ausgabe; ausführlichere Informationen können Sie im Internet unter www.dowani.com nachlesen. Alle eingespielten Versionen wurden live aufgenommen.

Die Klavierpädagogik hat in den letzten Jahren sehr große Fortschritte gemacht. Viele Klavierlehrer haben ihre eigenen Ideen, Theorien und Erfahrungen – vor allem in Bezug auf Fingersätze und die Verwendung des Pedals. Aus diesem Grund haben wir in dieser Ausgabe bewusst auf Fingersätze und Pedalanweisungen verzichtet.

Wir wünschen Ihnen viel Spaß beim Musizieren mit unseren *DOWANI 3 Tempi Play Along*-Ausgaben und hoffen, dass Ihre Musikalität und Ihr Fleiß Sie möglichst bald bis zur Konzertversion führen werden. Unser Ziel ist es, Ihnen durch Motivation, Freude und Spaß die notwendigen Voraussetzungen für effektives Üben zu schaffen.

Ihr DOWANI Team

# Concerto

for Piano and Orchestra, KV 415
C Major / Ut majeur / C-Dur

## I

W. A. Mozart (1756 – 1791)

DOW 17013

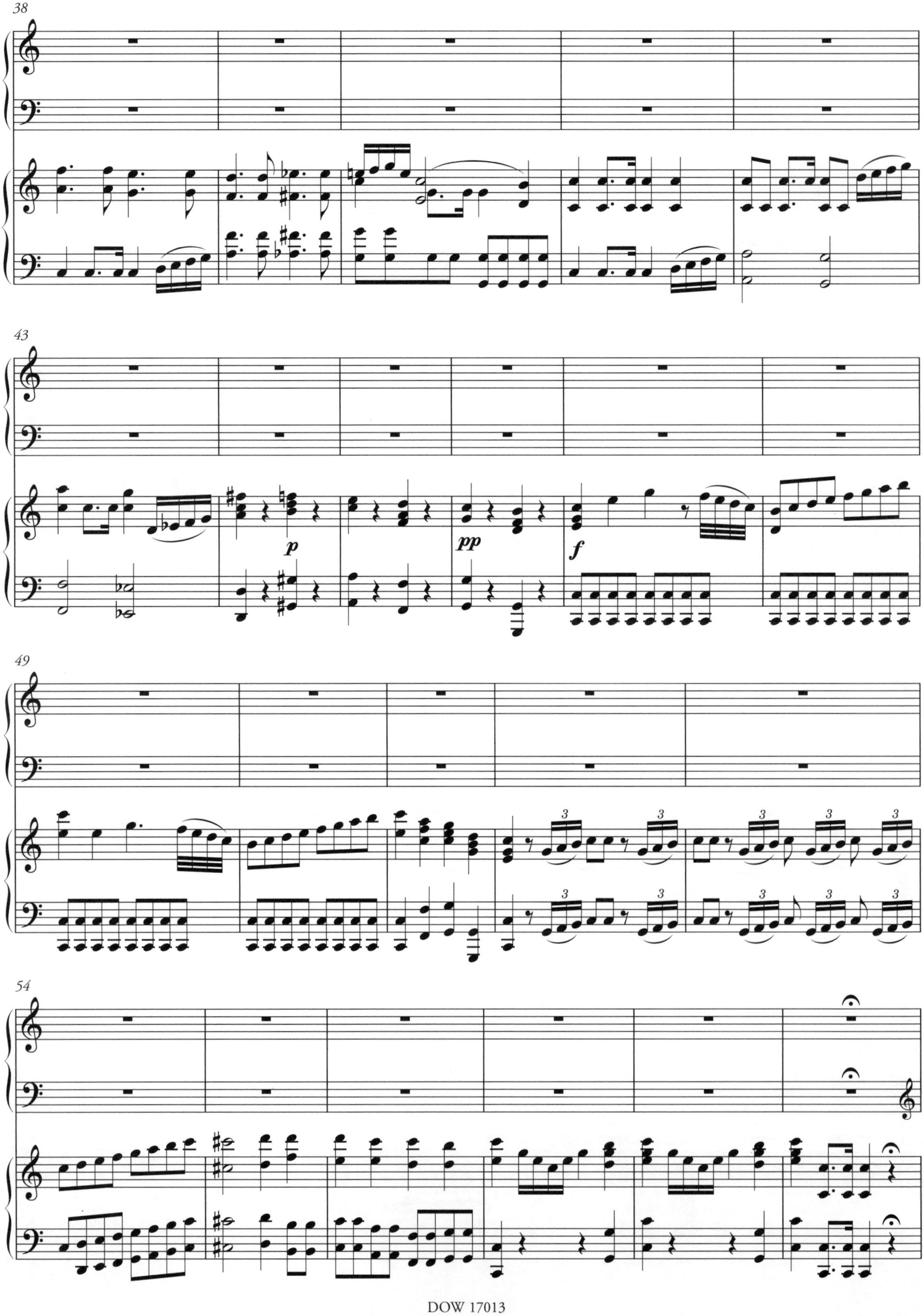
38
43
p
pp
f
49
3
54

10

Allegro

# II

# Wolfgang Amadeus
# MOZART

(1756 – 1791)

Concerto for Piano and Orchestra, KV 415
C Major / Ut majeur / C-Dur

Piano / Klavier

DOWANI International

# Concerto

### for Piano and Orchestra, KV 415
### C Major / Ut majeur / C-Dur

**I** A1

W. A. Mozart (1756 – 1791)

Cadenza

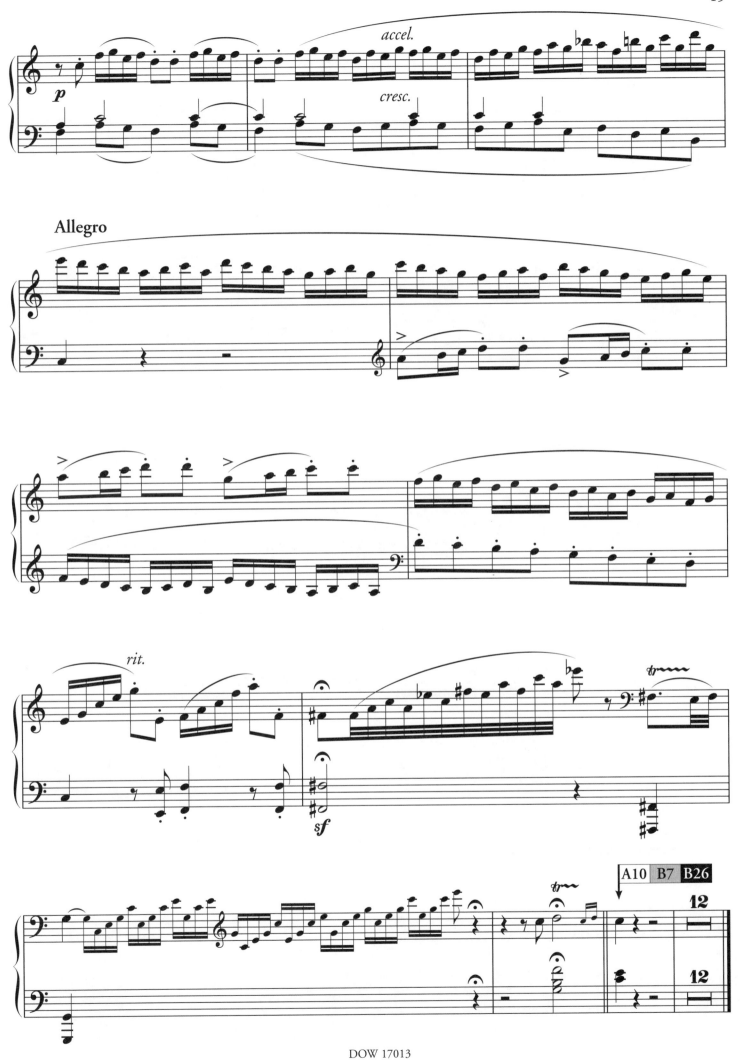

II

**Tempo I**

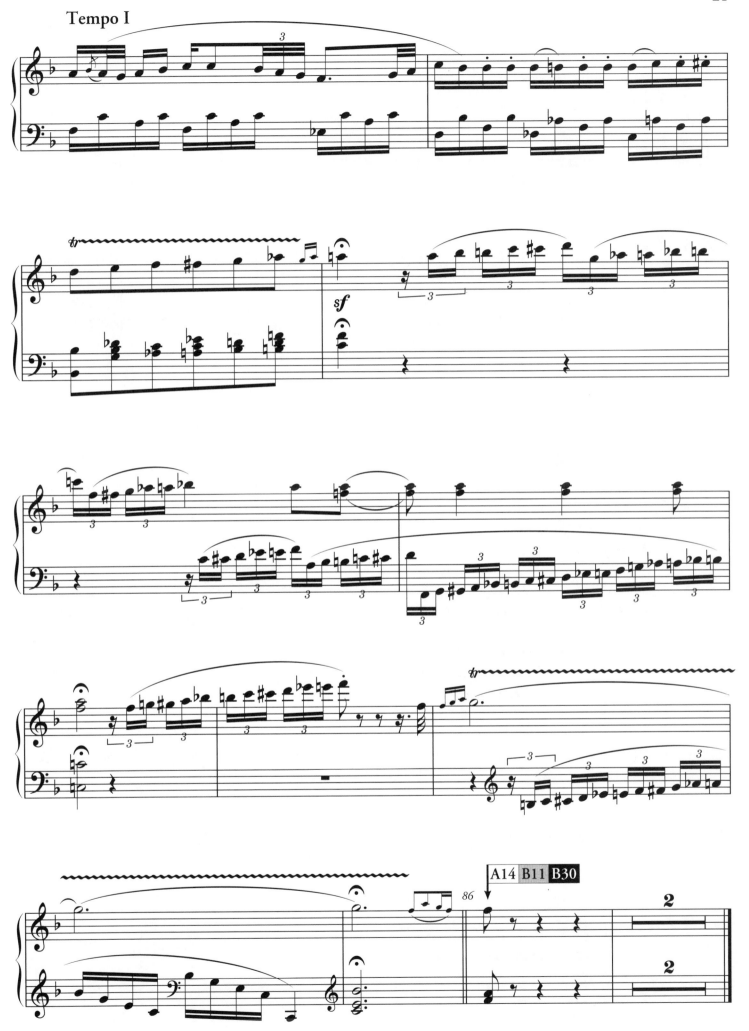

A14 B11 B30

22

Rondo

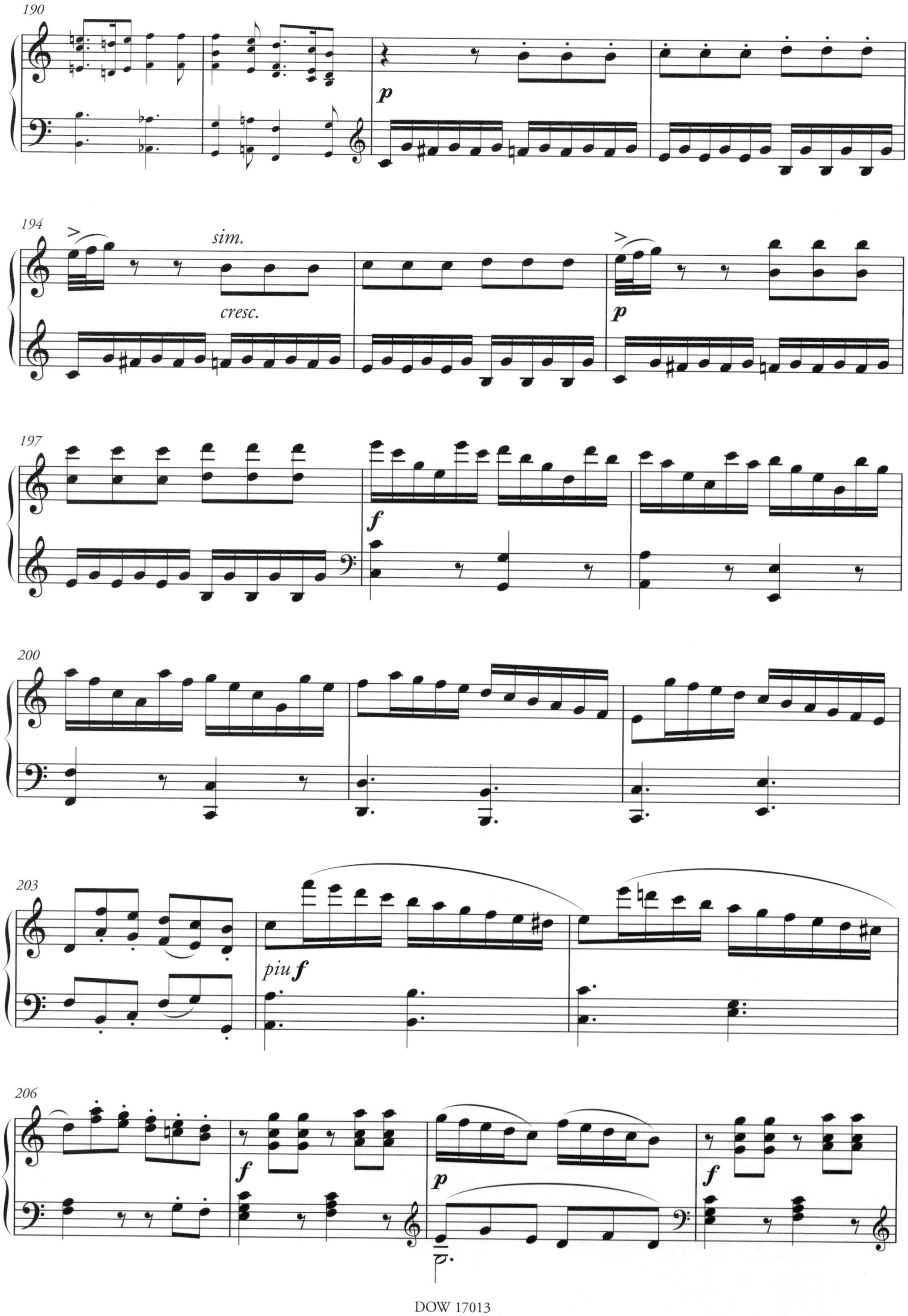
190
p
194
sim.
cresc.
p
197
f
200
203
piu f
206
f
p
f

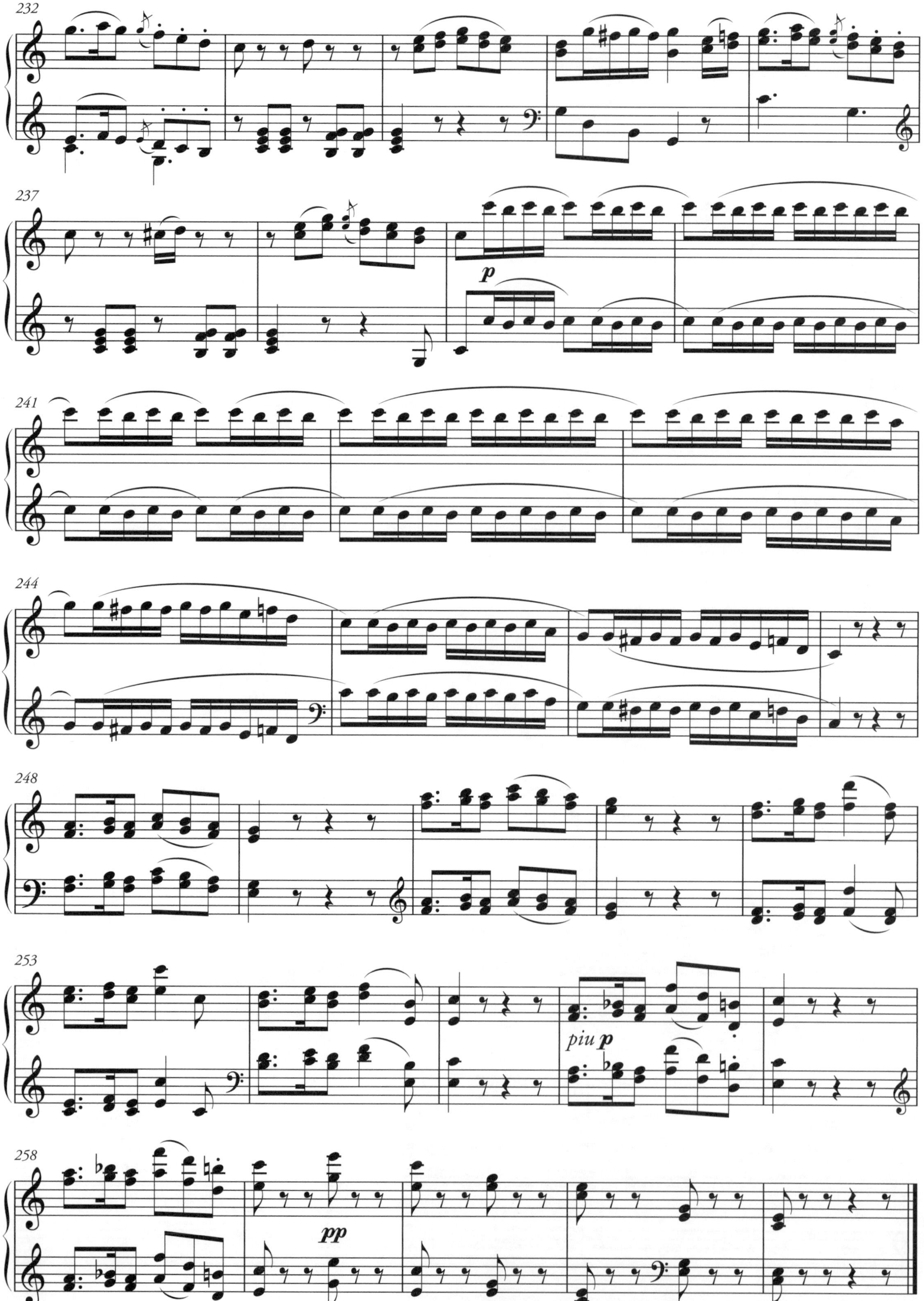
232
237
p
241
244
248
253
piu p
258
pp

# Rondo

**Allegro scherzando**

**Allegro scherzando**

*Eingang

## ENGLISH

DOWANI CD:

- Track numbers in circles          ⬤ - concert version

- Track numbers in squares          ▭ - slow Play Along Tempo

  - slow Play Along Tempo
  - intermediate Play Along Tempo
  - original Play Along Tempo

- Additional tracks for longer movements or pieces

- **Double CD:** CD1 = A, CD2 = B

- **Concert version:** piano and orchestra

- **Slow tempo:** channel 1: piano solo; channel 2: piano accompaniment; middle position: both pianos at the same volume

- **Intermediate tempo:** piano accompaniment only

- **Original tempo:** orchestra only

Please note that the recorded version of the piano accompaniment may differ slightly from the sheet music. This is due to the spontaneous character of live music making and the artistic freedom of the musicians. The original sheet music for the solo part is, of course, not affected.

Cadenzas: The full cadenzas are only played in the concert version.

## FRANÇAIS

DOWANI CD :

- N° de plage dans un cercle          ⬤ - version de concert

- N° de plage dans un rectangle       ▭

  - tempo lent play along
  - tempo moyen play along
  - tempo original play along

- Plages supplémentaires pour mouvements ou morceaux longs

- **Double CD :** CD1 = A, CD2 = B

- **Version de concert :** piano et orchestre

- **Tempo lent :** 1er canal : piano solo ; 2nd canal : accompagnement de piano ; au milieu : les deux pianos au même volume

- **Tempo moyen :** seulement l'accompagnement de piano

- **Tempo original :** seulement l'accompagnement d'orchestre

L'enregistrement de l'accompagnement de piano peut présenter quelques différences mineures par rapport au texte de la partition. Ceci est du à la liberté artistique des musiciens et résulte d'un jeu spontané et vivant, mais n'affecte, bien entendu, d'aucune manière la partie soliste.

Cadences : Les cadences entières ont été enregistrées seulement dans la version de concert.

## DEUTSCH

DOWANI CD:

- Trackangabe im Kreis          ⬤ - Konzertversion

- Trackangabe im Rechteck       ▭

  - langsames Play Along Tempo
  - mittleres Play Along Tempo
  - originales Play Along Tempo

- Zusätzliche Tracks bei längeren Sätzen oder Stücken

- **Doppel-CD:** CD1 = A, CD2 = B

- **Konzertversion:** Klavier und Orchester

- **Langsames Tempo:** 1. Kanal: Klavier solo, 2. Kanal: Klavierbegleitung, Mitte: beide Klaviere in gleicher Lautstärke

- **Mittleres Tempo:** nur Klavierbegleitung

- **Originaltempo:** nur Orchester

Die Klavierbegleitung auf der CD-Aufnahme kann gegenüber dem Notentext kleine Abweichungen aufweisen. Dies geht in der Regel auf die künstlerische Freiheit der Musiker und auf spontanes, lebendiges Musizieren zurück. Die Solostimme bleibt davon selbstverständlich unangetastet.

Kadenzen: Die Kadenzen sind nur in der Konzertversion komplett eingespielt.

**DOWANI - 3 Tempi Play Along is published by:**
DOWANI International
A division of De Haske (International) AG
Postfach 60, CH-6332 Hagendorn
Switzerland
Phone: +41-(0)41-785 82 50 / Fax: +41-(0)41-785 82 58
Email: info@dowani.com
www.dowani.com

**Recording & Digital Mastering:** Pavel Lavrenenkov, Russia
**Music Notation:** Notensatz Thomas Metzinger, Germany
**Design:** Andreas Haselwanter, Austria
**Printed by:** Zrinski d.d., Croatia
**Made in** Switzerland

**Concert Version**
Vitaly Junitsky, Piano
Russian Philharmonic Orchestra Moscow
Konstantin Krimets, Conductor

**3 Tempi Accompaniment**
**Slow**
Vitaly Junitsky, Piano

**Intermediate**
Vitaly Junitsky, Piano

**Original**
Russian Philharmonic Orchestra Moscow
Konstantin Krimets, Conductor